David
and his giant battle

janis hansen
illustrated by wendy francisco

CROSSWAY BOOKS • WHEATON, ILLINOIS
A DIVISION OF GOOD NEWS PUBLISHERS

ROBIN ROAD PRODUCTIONS
SHERMAN OAKS, CALIFORNIA

Dedicated
to all the little children of the world

OTHER BIBLE ADVENTURE CLUB STORIES

Creation: God's Wonderful Gift

Noah and the Incredible Flood

Jonah and His Amazing Voyage

Jesus: The Birthday of the King

David and His Giant Battle

Text and illustrations copyright © 2001 by Robin Road Productions

Published by Crossway Books, a division of Good News Publishers,

1300 Crescent Street, Wheaton, Illinois 60187

Illustrations: Wendy Francisco

First printing 2001

Printed in the United States of America

Library of Congress Cataloging-in-Publication Data
Hansen, Janis (Janis S.), 1942-
  David and his giant battle / Janis Hansen ; illustrated by
Wendy Francisco.
    p.   cm. - (Bible Adventure club)
  Summary: With his faith in God, David, a young shepherd,
defeats the Philistine giant Goliath.
  ISBN 1-58134-324-8 (alk. paper)
  1. David, King of Israel-Juvenile literature. [1. David, King of
Israel.
  2. Bible stories-O.T.] I. Francisco, Wendy, ill. II. Title.
BS580.D3 .H29   2001
222'.4309505-dc21   2001002270
                                                                 CIP
```
15  14  13  12  11  10  09  08  07  06  05  04  03  02  01
15  14  13  12  11  10   9   8   7   6   5   4   3   2   1
```

Welcome to David's Bible Adventure!

We're sure the kids in your life will love the journey they're about to embark on. From the great storybook and audio-cassette to the fun-filled activity book and interactive CD-Rom, your young adventurers will discover the story of *David* in a new and exciting way. And the "Parents' Guide" will help you play a vital role in their experience.

Because what and how kids learn is important to us, we've had every element of *David and His Giant Battle* reviewed by both a religious and an educational board of advisors. The content and vocabulary are appropriate for young children, and will help them develop reading and language skills, which are the cornerstones of education. Kids will also be able to expand and nourish their creativity as each Bible Adventure Club product challenges them to use their imagination. And most importantly, the knowledge they learn in these stories of God's Word will enhance their growing faith.

So begin with the great adventure stories of the Bible and start kids on a path that will enrich their lives in both faith and knowledge. And with you by their side, it'll be a fun-filled journey that you all will remember!

Even though Saul was king
of Israel, he had big problems.
He asked his most trusted servant for help.
  "I'm very unhappy! I feel like a black cloud is
covering my eyes. My head pounds with the pain
of a thousand hammers, and I have terrible dreams
every night!

"I need relief, but I don't know what to do!"

"Great king, I have heard of a boy in Bethlehem whose beautiful music is said to calm even wild animals. I'll send someone for him right away."

Far, far away from the king's troubles, it was a butterfly-and-bluebird kind of day.

A boy named David played his harp as he watched his father's sheep. The lambs and small creatures loved to hear him play. Suddenly David heard a lamb's frightened cry.

David jumped up and found himself face to face with a lion!

"Get away from that lamb! Pick on someone your own size!"

Without a second thought, David whapped the ferocious lion on the nose. The lion was so surprised that he ran away!

"Little lamb, you were very lucky today!
I don't even see a scratch!"

"David!"

"What, brother?"

"King Saul's messenger is waiting for you at
the house with father. He's going to take you to
the palace. Now don't worry; I'll watch the
sheep! Just go!"

"Father, what's going on?"
"David, the king needs you! Here are some snacks for your trip! You have to leave now!"

David and the messenger rode all night. As the
morning sun was rising, they arrived at the
palace where the king was waiting.

"David, our armies are constantly attacked by
the Philistines. The war just goes on and on.
I haven't slept for days, and I'm so tired! Perhaps
your music can bring me peace."

"I will gladly play for you, great king."

"I know God loves me; He keeps me safe,
Every day it's plain to see.
Thank You, dear God,
You're so good to me.
With God's love to guide me,
I feel so strong;
I'm as brave as I can be.
Thank You, dear God, You're so good to me.

I'm happy each day. I'm glad to be me.
Thank You, dear God, for my family.
Thank You for being so good to me."

King Saul loved David's music, so David played
for the king every day. Soon the king was well.
"David, you have helped me heal my mind.
Go home now to your family in Bethlehem."
"I'm happy I could serve you, my king."

"Father! I've missed you!"

"Oh, David, I'm glad you're home! But so much has happened!

"Your brothers are now in King Saul's army! Tomorrow take some breads and cheeses to their captain and see how they are doing."

As David neared the Israelite army camp, he heard the Israelites and the Philistine army shouting their battle cries at each other.

David searched through the soldiers and found his
brothers.

"Look who's here! It's David!"

"We're happy to see you!"

"We're getting all ready for the big fight tomorrow!"

Suddenly a silence fell over the Israelite
army. David and his brothers looked up and
saw a giant Philistine almost ten feet tall!

He shouted at the Israelites, "I am Goliath!
We don't need armies to fight each other.
Just send me one man to fight. If he wins, we
Philistines will be your servants. But if I win,
you Israelites will be our servants."

"This is terrible!"

"Only a fool would fight a giant."

"None of us Israelites is strong enough to go against Goliath!"

Not one of the soldiers was willing to fight Goliath. They were all afraid.

Then David spoke up.

"I will fight Goliath. I defended my father's sheep against lions and bears, and Goliath can be no worse!"

"That is totally foolish, David. You don't know what you're saying."

"David, don't even think about fighting that giant!"

Even King Saul tried to talk David out of fighting Goliath. "David, you are brave, but you cannot fight Goliath. He is a mighty warrior."

"My king, I may be a boy, but I am strong, and I have God on my side. With His help, I know I can strike Goliath down."

"Well, I can't argue with such faith, David. If you are set on doing it, at least let me give you my armor and a good sword."

David put on the king's heavy armor, and he picked up the sword.

"This armor is much too heavy for me. All I really need is my slingshot and five smooth stones."

When David stepped onto the battlefield to meet Goliath, the Philistines broke into loud laughter.

Goliath turned red with anger.

"You send a boy? To fight me?

How dare you insult me like this?

Boy, who are you to fight Goliath? Come here, and I will feed you to the buzzards!"

"My name is David, and I am a soldier of the Lord.

You have your weapons and your armor, but God has given me His power, and I am going to strike you down!"

Goliath was full of fury! He roared and ran toward David. David put a stone in his sling and bravely held his ground.

As Goliath raised his sword, ready to strike, David said a quick prayer:

"Please, God, give my arm strength and make my aim true."

He hurled the stone from his slingshot with all his might! The stone hit Goliath in the center of his forehead!

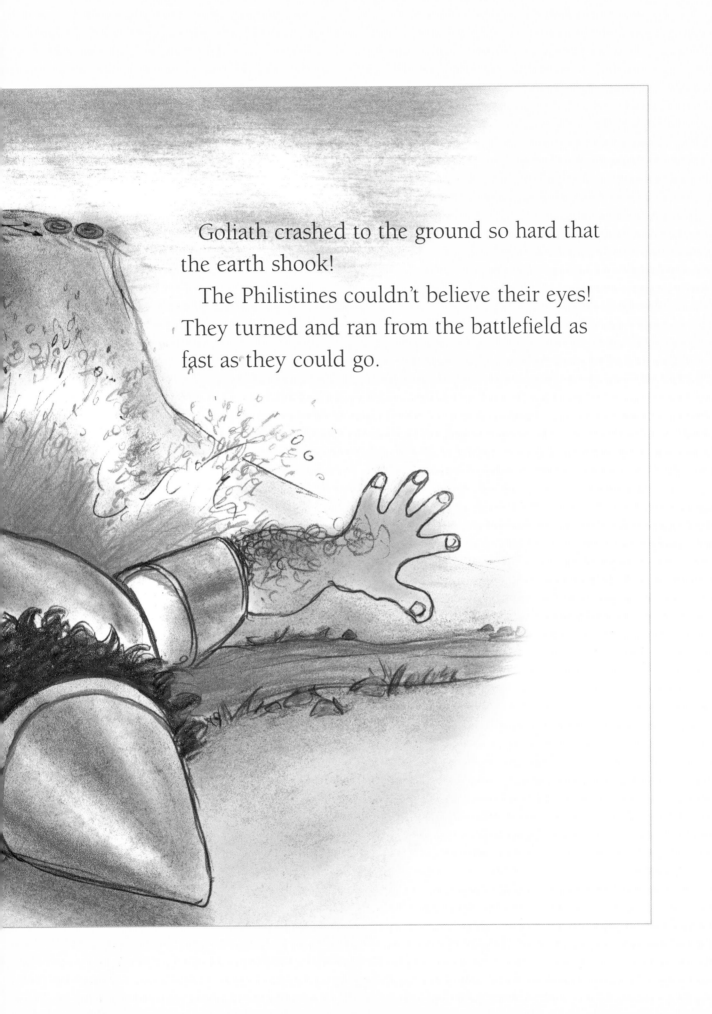

Goliath crashed to the ground so hard that the earth shook!

The Philistines couldn't believe their eyes! They turned and ran from the battlefield as fast as they could go.

The first thing David did was to give thanks to God.
"Thank you, God, for helping me save my people."
The Israelites crowded out onto the battlefield.
Everyone was cheering David!

Brave David later became one of the greatest kings of Israel.